Hood Healing, Thought Collection Publishing, and colophon are trademarks of Stellation Group, LLC.

THOUGHT COLLECTION PUBLISHING
P.O. Box 2132
Naperville, IL. 60540
www.thoughtcollection.org

Editing by Dena Chapman
Cover, Interior Design, and Illustration by Relana Johnson
Photography by Alex Callejo

First Edition, 2022
Print ISBN - 978-1-7334685-5-8
EPUB ISBN- 978-1-7334685-6-5

We hope you enjoy this book meant for expanding awareness and perspectives.

HoodHealing

INTERVIEWS WITH SOME OF
CHICAGO'S MOST PROLIFIC VOICES
IN MEDIA & BLACK CULTURE

Vee L. Harrison

FOREWORD BY DOMETI PONGO

Dedication

THIS **ART** IS FOR **MY ANCESTORS**.

THOSE I KNEW, AND TO THOSE I'VE YET TO MEET.

FOR **GRANDMA SHIRLEY** AND **SCOODA**,
WHO BOTH SPOKE CLEAR AS DAY TO ME WHILE WRITING THIS.

AND TO MAYA ANGELOU, TONI MORRISON,
WALTER DEAN MYERS, ZORA NEALE HURSTON,
LANGSTON HUGHES, MARCUS GARVEY, IDA B. WELLS,
JAMES BALDWIN, CONGRESSMAN JOHN LEWIS,
TUPAC SHAKUR, DMX, SANDRA BLAND,
LAQUAN MCDONALD, TRAYVON MARTIN,
MIKE BROWN, AND GEORGE FLOYD.

I FEEL AND HEAR ALL OF YOU, DEEPLY.

IN THE WIND, SUN, AIR, AND MY SOUL.

Table of Contents

Foreword

DOMETI PONGO

Journalist,
MTV News Correspondent
and Host of *"True Life Crime"*

"HOW MANY OF YOU HAVE BEEN PERSONALLY IMPACTED BY GUN VIOLENCE?"

Of the 30 teenagers to whom I posed this question, tucked away in a small classroom at a Southside Chicago-based community center, every single hand shot up. What followed was a conversation about how they've processed their losses - or even if they'd begun to; if they had the capacity to.

When I wasn't reporting on the same issues that viscerally impacted these kids, I was moonlighting as a youth counselor and media program instructor to offer young people creative alternatives to unhealthy life choices. Most days, it felt like we were getting somewhere. Other days, talking about the arts and shit in the middle of a war zone felt like a fool's errand.

The following year, another facilitator returns to this same classroom to pose a similar question. This time, one less hand shoots up.

Not because there's a new student here who was lucky enough to escape the trauma that ensnares so many of Chicago's babies.

Quite the opposite. Terry isn't in class this summer. He was killed just weeks after last summer's term ended.

The questions must delve a little deeper now. How can we begin to address the trauma associated with becoming accustomed to something so abnormal as premature loss? How can we bring healing to the hood?

Enter Vee Harrison. I first spoke with the Westside-bred journalist in the Spring of 2020 when she interviewed me to contribute to a now-viral piece she'd written for the Black-woman-owned outlet TRiiBE.com. It was titled, *"A West Side House Party Exposes the Disconnect between Young Black Residents, Chicago Officials, and the News During COVID-19 Pandemic"* and underscored the level of care, raw authenticity, and connection to the community that informs this book.

Hood Healing

At the onset of the corona virus pandemic amid lockdown orders, a 26-year-old Black woman threw a packed, maskless kickback sparking outrage amid the spread of a then-mysterious airborne virus. When pictures of the Westside house party hit the internet, the fallout was widespread and immediate, with every outlet from TMZ to CNN clamoring to cover the story of the inner-city partiers who put lives at risk. There was a subtle racially-tinged air in many of these dog-whistle-filled reports.

Harrison's coverage put into words what Black Chicagoans from disinvested neighborhoods were thinking but couldn't quite articulate. "Why do they care about us now?"

Without dismissing the gravity of the offense (there were more than 48,000 statewide cases at the time), her work at The TRiiBE highlighted the subtle hypocrisy undergirding the conversation, the fact that much of the scolding came from the same figureheads and institutions that have maligned Chicago's Black communities for decades.

Independent of one's opinions of the event itself, I was struck by this writer's commitment to nuance and the amplification of voices that have long been omitted from these conversations. Unfortunately, that omission over time has quite literally culminated in a dangerous information gap as more people of color disengage from mainstream media.

The tone and perspective of writers like Harrison are refreshing to anyone who's felt the news cover their environment from a bird's eye view. Out of touch reporters parachute in for the sensational headlines before fleeing to the comfort of their television screens to scold communities for living in the beds others have made for them. They don't know what it's like to walk in those shoes. To sleep in those beds.

Shortly after reaching out to ask me to join *Hood Healing*, Harrison shared the devastating news that her brother was killed. I asked if she needed time to pause her project. She told me," No." Instead, the trauma strengthened her resolve to delve deeper into this work. That's how important this undertaking is. The text is as cathartic for the writer as it is for the reader. It won't be politically correct, and it shouldn't be. For there is no lesson in constant correctness. Blind optimism doesn't adorn these pages. Rather, these pages will remind us to find the beauty in our experiences, the strength to overcome what didn't kill us, and the confidence to celebrate the scars the hood gave us.

For they are the evidence of our ability to heal.

Dometi Pongo

Hood Healing

Chapter One

COUSINS, CORNERS, COFFINS & COPS

FEATURING EVAN F. MOORE
Author, Chicago Sun-Times Arts and Culture Reporter

I THINK I FIRST TRAUMA EXPERIENCED WHEN I WAS EIGHT-YEARS OLD.

I lived on the West Side of Chicago, and I remember being in my living room and witnessing my momma and daddy randomly burst out of the bathroom, my momma grabbing my daddy telling him not to leave. I remember my momma being in only her bra and jeans, a black bra, and afterward, after daddy had left anyway, seeing her check the small candy jars and random places for change. Momma seemed to be scrambling to see if we had money in the house. I remember her not finding much...

I remember being scared. And nosey. I wanted to know what was happening, without asking questions. In that moment, I was more worried about my momma, but I also remember wondering where my daddy had to be that was so important to him.

I hadn't witnessed scenes like that often in my home. But I didn't need to. That one instance was enough content for me.

I think it wasn't until my adulthood that I connected that trauma to my dad's then drug habit. It wasn't until a few years ago that I had even considered that exchange to be a traumatic experience. I had buried it deep inside because although I was only eight, I knew the significance of what took place, but I had no understanding of why it was happening.

Nobody spoke to me about it—what I saw or what had happened. Nobody seemed to wonder if afterward, I was confused or had questions. It was likely too complex to explain, and for me, it was definitely too uncomfortable to ask.

Like our ancestors' wombs, the hood is full of broken Black babies with unanswered and unasked questions. And like our ancestors' souls, the hood is haunted with dark breaths, deep alleys, dark alleys, and deep breaths...

The hood made us feel pretty unwanted, but we all got used to that. The fact that Black families were unwanted was nearly the only thing that wasn't a secret in the family. Everything else was family business.

Hood Healing

When you grow up Black, family secrets become a part of your life. And the inner-city hoods, the blocks in which we grow up are the places those secrets play out. But as life is happening, we seldom connect what happened to us, to what is currently happening to us. What I do know is this: the internal burying of such traumatic scenes is what felt so natural. I learned it from my ancestors; burying pain in the pit of your gut is what they knew to do. They didn't know this term then, but it's called *masking*.

Masking is like magic: poof! In our mind we check out, just disappear.

Dr. Tanya Sorrell, a Black Psychology and Psychiatry Professor at Chicago's Rush University, helped me connect the trauma to our psyches. See, what I do know is that some critic somewhere isn't deeming my own traumatic experiences as expert enough to sell on Amazon. Some critics may say that at 34-years-old, I've barely experienced enough life to share a story of healing from ancestral pain.

Sure.

That is why on a sunny day in Chicago, Dr. Sorrell and I had lunch to talk about how these things all come together as psychological and psychiatric trauma. Not so much to prove to y'all that I know what I'm talking about and I know where to get information, but to better connect my past trauma to my current life, and to discover why I'm so dedicated to this book.

"I think my perspective adds a lens that is slightly different because I am not a native Chicagoan; I'm from Louisiana," Dr. Sorrell explained to me. *"I knew of people who went up North in that great migration. I knew of people that went out West as part of that great migration. My uncle and aunt were part of that great migration to California."*

Dr. Sorrell said that although she grew up in Louisiana, the picture of inner-city Chicago was already painted for her well before she arrived. National news outlets, like CNN, have headlined Chicago's violent and impoverished conditions in the inner city's neighborhoods. The people who reside in these neighborhoods are typically Black, Hispanic, and poor. Neighborhoods like Austin, where I grew up, were dirty and destitute. Our parks had glass on the grounds and needles in phone booths left behind by heroin addicts. My five siblings and I went to schools where the teachers had to manage the amount of toilet paper we used in the bathrooms because there was never enough to accommodate the entire school population. Nor were there enough books, so we shared books during out-loud reading time.

What Dr. Sorrell had learned about Chicago before living and working here helped broaden her understanding and perspective of Black trauma inside the soul of the city.

"I don't just see the surface issues, which is what is frequently reported, but I see past that. We may only feel that band-aids are being placed on things that are multiple layers thicker than the issues at the surface."

As Dr. Sorrell puts it, *we're just masking, not living beyond the surface.*

I've been masking for years. Just like the rest of y'all.

And I'm masking because growing up Black, sharing your pain could get you talked about, clowned by your people, whooped, or sometimes lectured by momma about not telling folks "what's going on in my house."

Masking came from our ancestral makeup. Keeping quiet, being docile. Not trusting nobody. Abused. Silenced.

Our ancestors didn't have the luxury of processing their pain. And because of this, their pain has passed through our blood and our trauma has sat still in the wombs of Black mothers on welfare, on the hearts of Black daddies in custody courts, and on the minds of Black kids looking to escape their pain with Xanax and brown liquor.

Growing up in the hood wasn't the time or place to share your family secrets. And when there's barely resources to feed you and your family, a mental health facility is hard to come by, even by imagination. As vital as it is to dump our emotions and share them with a therapist, so often communities of color lack mental health facilities and resources to do just that. Furthermore, this whole idea of not sharing family business made therapy seem unreal and unattainable. Healing and overcoming our trauma seemed to be just a figment of our imaginations.

Speaking of imagination, what always blew my mind about the hood was that people talked so much about getting out, yet my eyes saw people trapped on the blocks that they tried so hard to escape. The blocks where I literally saw folks making raps, were the same blocks I saw them memorializing one another with teddy bears and cognac. So, it seemed to me that this idea of getting out of the hood was just that: an idea. A figment of the hood's imagination. A hope with no plan. A goal with no realistic parameters.

Black people in Chicago know a thing or five about hopes with no plans.

Hood Healing

The West Side was my home, right near Chicago Avenue and Austin where the streetlights separated the haves and have-nots from a community riddled with poverty, food deserts, and crime (Austin) on one side of the street, and a community known for its architectural heritage and elegant restaurants (Oak Park) on the other side. The hood, for me, was only what I saw from my bedroom window of our two-story home. My momma was scared of the streets, scared to lose us, and scared as hell to die out there. So oftentimes, we created opportunities right in our home to have fun, cheap fun. My momma would make us playdough with flour dough and she'd make homemade bubbles out of dish detergent, using a pan and spatula to make bubbles that floated all through the house. She was perfect at taking care of us; we always had what we needed. We thought we were lacking, but we really lacked nothing at all.

My daddy was a car salesman, and a victim of the 1980's crack epidemic. Family chatter says that he cleaned himself up when my younger twin sisters were born. He figured it was time to rid himself of what would eventually be the pain borne by his 16 grandchildren; the patriarchal pains of carrying generations on your back showed in my dad and was reflective of being let down by countless life mistakes - some his own, many he couldn't control...

Seeing the different types of Black men from my city was something I studied, even as a child. Growing up, the men in my family ranged from crackheads to mechanics. We had family members who were pretty well off, an uncle who cut hair that the whole hood knew, and family members who crashed on our living room couches for years at a time.

Following Dr. Martin Luther King Jr.'s death in 1968, the West Side (including neighborhoods like North Lawndale where King and his family once lived) was already suffering from disinvestment, just like the South Side. So, in 2020, after the murder of George Floyd, which sparked a barrage of nationwide protests and riots, neither the West Side nor the South Side of Chicago could afford another beatdown. Of more concern and frustration was the fact that there was little to no data or statistics on what contributed to the demise of these impoverished urban communities of color.

I remember covering this very issue in a hyperlocal publication I helped pioneer during college, AustinTalks. At that time, I had interviewed Marsha Belcher, the Director of Marketing and Research at the Community and Economic Development Association of Cook County.

"The Austin area does not have a lot of options for young moms to purchase fresh vegetables, fruits, and dairy for their babies at affordable prices," said Marsha Belcher.

That story ran in 2011. That was just a year after an Aldi's in Oak Park was demolished and replaced with a recreational center. That Aldi's was the nearest and most affordable place for Black families in Austin, including mine, to put food in front of their families. In the hood, we were used to seeing things like that happen often; the closure of healthcare facilities, grocery stores, and schools. The trauma of losing our essential things seemed to be okay with the local government.

By that time in 2011, my family and I had moved on from the city...and to most of my friends, we had "moved on up". I've never forgotten one of my closest friends called on the day we moved to Bellwood, signaling me to take notice that we had an upstairs and downstairs. It was reflective of how little we had before, and how little so many of our friends and family had, as well.

We had people thinking we had made it. But not really...

Chicago was still a part of our lives. Our family. Our meat market. My educational foothold was Columbia College, where I eventually received my B.A. in Journalism. The city was our crib. But it's almost like we didn't want much to do with it anymore. We had tried to not make it look like that, but it was like that. My momma was pretty blatant about the city being a dump, and it was. The local cops were known for harassing and sometimes killing the very people that looked like us or lived with us. So, this sense of "serve and protect" didn't exist in the hood. And in an environment like Chicago where Black people need to heal, it didn't make it easier for us to seek healing when we witnessed those sent to serve and protect, actually harassed and killed the people that look like us.

The Nationwide Police Scorecard, a report originated by researchers and professors at Columbia University, UC Irvine, and the University of Oxford, recently ranked the Chicago Police Department as the second-worst police department in the country. Researchers and professors found that our city's cops solved fewer homicides than 88% of police departments across the nation. My brother's murder is of that unsolved 88%. While Chicago's local media tends to count the deceased bodies, the stories connecting the bodies to the long history of trauma remains untold.

My only brother, Darryl, was killed earlier this year. Now gone forever, his tragic, traumatic story remains untold. Right behind his house out west, he was shot ten times in the alley and left to bleed out in the snow. Cold and crawling for his life. Blood leaving his body, like our daddy leaving him home with momma during his childhood to roam the streets for his next heroin high. His body freezing cold and alone, like my momma felt when she carried him in her 17-year-old womb, unsure of his fate. Unsure of how to raise him with a sick man who wasn't strong enough for his manhood. And nearly 40 years later, my momma got a call she was in no way ready to receive.

Neither was I.

My brother died in a hood that isn't fair to anyone. And that's the norm in Chicago. It's regular news; consistent content of killings, rape, disappearances. So much of Chicago is covered in the news, but so often, it's the same ole report. The news has yet to emphasize the generational trauma steeped in violence and murder; the murders of Black people, Black men, like my brother, Darryl.

In the words of Evan F. Moore, *Chicago Sun-Times* Arts, and Culture Reporter, *"People will write about your community, and not include you."*

I interviewed Evan for this book because I knew two things for certain: he's a Black storyteller of the culture, and he's from the hood.

Vee: *What do you remember about your experience growing up in the hoods of Chicago?*

Evan: *I grew up on the South Side in the South Shore neighborhood in a two-parent household. Both of my parents were CPS [Chicago Public Schools] educators. I grew up in a family where pretty much immediate and extended family lived in South Shore or a nearby area. Growing up, I would hear a lot of different stories about things going on in the neighborhood and the world. Things like killings of Black people, wars, all types of stuff. I was a quiet kid, more of an observer. I would hear stories about Black life not only in Chicago but nationwide. My family were activists, teachers, social workers, small business owners, members of the Nation of Islam, and also the Black Panther Party and did all types of community things. It was always instilled in me to be involved in my community.*

Vee: *How do you define the hood? What does that mean to you?*

Evan: *I always tell people that growing up in South Shore, even to this day, it's one of the most diverse neighborhoods in the city. When you speak of diversity in normal terms, you think of race and economics. On my block alone, we had a former football player that got into finance and he'd ride around the hood in* his Ferrari. We had Black teachers, a CTA bus driver. We had different types of folks doing different things. You saw that. Even the police lived in our hoods. Our first interaction with the police officers was through our parents, the coaches. Think about it. Usually, the first interaction for Black people with a police officer is a negative one. It was weird...We also had people in our neighborhood who were doing pretty well for themselves, and then people who needed government assistance, like stamps and such. Growing up, my family was nicknamed the Huxtables because I was growing up in a couple of different worlds. That's kinda heavy for a kid to think about when people around you are like, 'Why do you talk this way or act that way?'

Vee: What are things you remember growing up in your home that prepared you to deal with the traumas of Chicago?

Evan: In our household, we grew up with a lot of Black-faced figurines. Over time, I noticed that they would be near the door. So, I asked my mom what was up with that. She was like this is a reminder for you that every time you leave the world, this is what white people think of you. She kinda spoon-fed us an extremely heavy lesson. And when you look at what's going on in the world, mom was right. She still is right. When you think about how certain folks are treated around the world, particularly Black folks, and a subset of that, Black women, you realize that the game, no matter where you go and what you do, the game is rigged. I'm someone that grew up in a two-parent household, went to a good college, has two Masters degrees, and also when it was my time to have interaction with the police or other folks being threatened about my presence in their space, nobody cared about those things.

Vee: If you were to identify one thing in Chicago and say that this is why this city struggles the way that it does, what is that element and why?

Evan: I would say just the lack of positive things to do in our communities. One of my last articles from the Sun-Times was about those spaces in Chicago way back in the 90s when kids were into hip-hop and everything else. When you think about it, those spaces aren't around anymore. There's not a whole lot for kids to do.

That kinda plays into your article that you wrote last year with The TRiiBE with that huge house party. People were like 'How can they do this?' Don't they listen, this, that, and the third. The person you quoted was like "Yeah, I know about this, [COVID 19] but it's not a whole lot for us to do." The systemic issues in the community were only made worse because of COVID. I think that's one major problem, lack of spaces for kids just to be kids. When you see the local news,

Hood Healing

people driving around our community and saying things like why are people in the park or doing this, that, and the third? Like shit, look around. Ain't shit for them to do. Where the fuck you think they're going to go? This is not science.

It isn't science. Studying the interactions between these factors: the government, the media, and the hood, it's more like social studies.

What Evan is referring to, is the story that made my career. The story was about a Chicago house party on the West Side that made national news for exposing the disconnect between young Black residents, Chicago officials, and the news during the COVID-19 pandemic *(The TRiiBE,* April 29, 2020). TMZ reported that the house party had 1,000 young people in attendance during the height of the pandemic. The implication made was that in the face of the pandemic, the Black young people who initiated and attended this party were irresponsible and reckless.

In my story, I discussed the disconnect between local law enforcement, the media, and the young people out west at that house party. My story revealed why the disconnect happened: when your neighborhood neglects you, and both the local and worldwide news only shows people who look like you in a negative light, what is there to trust?

Now, combine that disconnect and that distrust, to generations of degrading treatment, poor neighborhoods, inequitable healthcare, and a lack of incentive to teach Black children about the greatness of their history and who they are. The devastating result is layers of unresolved trauma. And the disconnect is purposeful, and a result of our ancestors' enslavement.

Chapter Two

HISTORY, HIGHWAYS, HYPES & HOPE

FEATURING GARRARD MCCLENDON
Emmy Award-Winning Journalist and Author

300 YEARS LATER···
TRASH···
EVERYWHERE!

It's an eyesore in Black inner-city hoods across this whole nation. When you reside in communities like Englewood, Garfield Park, Little Village, and North Lawndale, it's not uncommon to walk out your front door and be greeted by trash. On local school grounds, there's trash. On the highways to connect the hoods, more trash. And the issue of trash everywhere is not just an inner-city concept that starts and ends in Chicago. I'm talking about everywhere there are predominantly Black or Brown people, there's an overabundance of trash littering our hoods. Baltimore, Maryland, Miami Gardens, Florida. Flint, Michigan. Gary, Indiana. TRASH!

This is not a coincidence. Nor are the outdated school buildings, and the living conditions in which Black people are relegated and expected to accept. In neighborhoods only blocks away, things are vastly different; clutter is not king and people are living much better.

"Check out the expressway, when you go from the Kennedy to downtown, to the Dan Ryan. The further South you go from downtown to the Dan Ryan, the more trash you see on the side of the road," explained Garrard McClendon, award-winning journalist and tv show host from Chicago.

I interviewed Garrard because I truly needed the voice of someone from the industry who covered Chicago before me; the old-school perspective was necessary.

I asked Garrard what was up with the trash in Chicago, and what did this type of life say to Black youth in Chicago?

"It tells you that you're worthless. I'm worth trash. My neighborhood is filled with trash," Garrard answered.

I knew that although I was surrounded by trash in a trashy hood, I wasn't trash. At least I thought I knew I wasn't trash. However, when we're trapped inside of a system, our mentality clings to that system. See, I wasn't trash, but I still was near it enough to know it.

I was near it enough to see crackheads out my window, outdated cafeterias inside of disenfranchised school buildings with molded walls, and broken bathroom stall doors. At home, I was cared for, but things around me weren't. Like Evan in South Shore, I was a part of two different worlds; my world was out west, in Austin.

The trauma from constantly being surrounded by trash isn't talked about enough. Picture this: our enslaved ancestors being transported to an unfamiliar land in feces-infested ships bound by the ankle. Same picture, though in a different frame. The picture shifts from slave ships to disinvested neighborhoods. Garrard explained to me some of this disinvestment and the unhealed trauma that contributes to it:

Vee: *What are some things that you believe are contributing to trauma in Chicago?*

Garrard: *Black people are being treated like the same trash that's covering our neighborhoods. In some of these neighborhoods, the fast-food restaurants use grease for five or six days before they even throw it out. And everybody says, 'Oh, that chicken tasted good.' Yeah, it tastes good; the grease is eight days old! What happens is you start getting used to something that is detrimental to you. When something becomes an everyday occurrence for you, whether it's being mistreated, or being lied to by a politician, whether it's not having adequate facilities or textbooks in a school system, or getting laptop computers six weeks later than everyone else, that's telling that child, you're worthless.*

This idea of worthlessness and lack of security and intelligence dates back to the early 1800s.

Something that Dr. Sorrell taught me during our time together at lunch is the connection between racism and psychiatry. She told me that she recently developed a talk that is now required for all medical providers enrolled in new courses at Rush University. The talk is based on the development of psychiatry and how from the very beginning, it has had that same type of white supremacist base. Dr. Sorrell said:

"The first things we are taught in psychiatry are the study of the brain and the study of the mind -phrenology – where we felt then we could tell what someone's intelligence, their mental and emotional capabilities were by the size and protrusion of their skull. And so, what did we see at that time? We saw pictures of white males that had pronounced frontal lobes, which we thought was the higher level of intelligence, which it is. And we saw pictures of Black people that were more caricatured to look more like apes and primates. And so, that actually gave the impression that the Black head and Black skull is not as developed on the frontal lobes; so the cognition, the higher-level thinking, and the intelligence is not there. We frequently saw pictures during those times where they showed the side view of an African-American next to the side view of a primate. This was right during the time of Darwin's evolution theory where it played into the evolution from a primate, to Black, and to whites. It played right into the thought that there was mental inferiority in Black people."

Frederick Douglass was said to be intelligent, and one of the very few prominent Black leaders of his time. He is credited with high intelligence and being articulate because he was the product of a white slave master (who raped his mother) making him half-white. In essence, he had white in his blood, and back then, that gave him a seat at the table.

As a mother of biracial children through a biracial marriage, I wonder just how far we've come from these thought processes? How far have we traveled down history with the belief that lighter skin tone, straight hair texture, culture affiliation, tribe names, and mixed babies really aren't offensive?

Not too far...considering I've been called whitewashed after marrying a white man. And I was officially told that groups like the Hebrew Israelites wouldn't accept my half-white babies due to their hate of "the white man". Although my children are products of my Black womb, they are what their white father is; so my children aren't Black. I guess me "of all people" shocked my haters after learning I was with a white man. I guess to some folks, that makes me "less Black", and perhaps less qualified to write this book.

Sure.

Trauma within begins with circumstances outside, most of which are outside of one's control. What can be controlled, however, is the narrative of Black people. What we can do is preserve the history which we do know. We can begin to document what it is, and what it was, for the African diaspora and its future generations.

Hood Healing

So, I asked Garrard something I had been wondering about for decades. A question that really digs down to the roots of who we are as descendants of African slaves: the truth.

Vee: *Historically, before my lifetime and before your lifetime, too, there was this richness and this elegance and value of what Africans stood for, who we were. What happened to that Black?*

Garrard: *When you look at the 60s and early 70s, it was more profitable for a sistah to not have a man...think about that. I'd have a baby with you, but please don't stick around, because I have no check anymore...that becomes problematic - clearly, a systematic design by the Nixon administration.*

When you look at the evolution of music and art in this country, specifically after the golden age of hip-hop when everything started moving toward the nefarious activity of killing people and drug selling, that became normal. We see it with a lot of Chicago rappers who have been murdered over the last few years, and if you listen to the rap songs, the songs are a prayer. The killings look like it's within, but it's without. There's a lack of opportunity, but some people don't know how to get out.

Vee: *How do we begin the journey of healing the hood?*

Garrard: *The people of power know what it takes, but are they willing to sacrifice for what the city needs? If you have 80% employment on the South and West sides, the entire city of Chicago will be a yellow brick road; people will walk with their heads up. That's the one thing that politicians and the wealthy can actually make happen in Chicago. But they don't want to do that because of selfishness. And we see that on the national scale with 49 republican senators who did not vote for a $1400 check for United States citizens. How petty can you be?*

To get to a place of healing, we have to one, forgive ourselves, two, forgive those around us, and three, get to work! However, what I hear when I speak to people is a lack of forgiveness. 'I blame my momma. I blame my daddy.' And because we don't have adequate therapy, a therapeutic construct, and a system in our communities, it becomes even worse. You can't even get out what you need to get out. Child molestation, poverty, lack of education...bad things that have to be forgiven before you can move forward. You gotta let that trauma go. It's hard to do, it's hard to process. But you have to let it go to move forward. To escape the trauma, you need to forgive yourself and you need to get with a mentor as quickly as possible; someone that you aspire to be, that's living an edifying and legal lifestyle.

Garrard continues to work his way through his own trauma after losing his parents to a brutal murder in Chicago in October of 2019. During his TV career at CLTV/WGN, he learned that his parents were murdered and found in a forest preserve. He learned this only minutes before going on the air...

"The murder was due to a home invasion, and due to two, young Black Gangster Disciples who decided to break into my parents' home and take them captive. They took everything they had, bound them, tied them up, put them in the closet, left, came back, killed them, took them to the forest preserve, and dumped them. I'm not special, nobody is. I will never completely get over that. How could I?"

Garrard shared that he grieves his parents daily, just like he grieves every child that is taken by violence in Chicago, or anywhere in the world.

"Violence is literally killing generations, and I could never be okay with that," Garrard said. *"That's why the media needs to report on this stuff. Black people dying in the streets will never be normal for me. We have got to start talking about what this is really about."*

It was nearing the first year of a pandemic that had killed more Black people in Chicago than any other racial group in the city. But that isn't what took my brother, Darryl. Even with preexisting conditions, he had managed to dodge the pandemic, but he couldn't escape murder in the alley behind his house.

"Murders should be rare, Vee. The fact that both of us have lost loved ones to homicide is just beyond the pale. If you ask 100 people 'Do you know of anyone that has been murdered?' One or two out of 100, should be able to tell you yes. These days, if you ask 100 people, 'Do you know of anyone who has been murdered?' 96 or 97 people will tell you yes."

The grief that Chicagoans experience spans from highway to highway and from corner to corner, yet the national coverage only reveals half the story. The media doesn't always tell the story of how this trauma is the same as our ancestors. And the way we bury the trauma is the same way that they did. If we don't intentionally heal the pain and the grief and the betrayal of millions, we only perpetuate the vicious cycle of trauma and prolong our healing.

Chapter Three

FAMILY, FRIENDS, FOES & FACEBOOK

FEATURING SANDRA HARRISON
CEO of DVA Training and Development Consultants
and My Momma

PASSING DOWN FAMILY TRAUMA
IN THE HOOD MOST TIME GOES UNSEEN,
BECAUSE IN MOST CASES, WE DON'T REALIZE THAT
OUR OWN FAMILIES
ARE CREATING TRAUMA ALL AROUND US.

Most residents of Chicago don't consider that to be what's happening on the streets. I felt like the older I got, the harder it was to understand the trauma and where it all began. Inside of my home was an obvious place to begin. However, my momma did such a good job at making the trauma we experienced look alright. Most times, she skillfully dressed up my family's trauma. The trauma I wore was always dressed to the nines; no one could tell that the trauma my siblings and I wore was from the Goodwill and Salvation Army stores. The walls inside of my Chicago home only expanded the trauma that was trapped inside of me. My siblings and I mainly had one another, and not much recreation outside of our home. And when you're with your siblings all the time, they become enemies and then homies again by nighttime.

We defined family as the people that lived in the house with us. In our community, that could be cousins, homeless uncles, and aunts, displaced friends, evicted children. You could say that our house was pretty cramped; for me, it felt like what I imagined the living quarters on a slave ship to be. Housing in Chicago is yet another root and leaf to Black trauma. In the early 1960's, the inner-city housing projects were reminiscent of revamped slave ships, only this time with concrete walls, roaches, and daily domestic disputes. Black people in Chicago were once again metaphorically piled up on top of one another, but as distant from one another as any other ethnic group - or so it seemed. Even in the smallest, confined, filthy places, these conditions were a set-up for trauma to seep through the cracks and spill over into the family's bloodline. That's because with Black people, trauma is in our blood.

"The first traumatic experience I can recall is the one that I often talk about;

Hood Healing

it's the recollection of my momma shooting my daddy," said Sandra Harrison, longtime Chicago resident, entrepreneur, and my momma.

What my momma shared with me were things that I had heard bits and pieces of, but the full story never added up. That's mainly because our parents spend so many years unpacking their own pain that they tend to hurt us in the process. My momma unpacked decades of her pain in what was nearly a two-hour FaceTime interview I had anxiously scheduled with her. She shared stories of her relationship with my daddy, her siblings, and her parents. And listening to some of the things she told me made me feel like I didn't truly know my momma.

"I had to be about 6-years-old and my dad had been gone for a year already," Momma said. *"Our friends would talk about my parents. I could be jumping rope and they'd be singing songs about my parents' messed up relationship. In those moments, I had no idea that their relationship was causing me trauma. I learned to live through it."*

My momma shared in-depth her upbringing with my grandma, which was so much like my own life that I literally felt deep inside of my own self as I wrote this book. In other words, I embodied that trauma.

Vee: *Can you tell me more about your mother, (my grandma) and more about your upbringing as a child?*

Momma: *I don't have a vantage point in my lifetime where I ever saw my mother as the bad guy; I don't have that perspective so I can't speak to that. I can certainly speak to my experiences later in life, like, being in the backseat of the car while my momma was driving down the street chasing somebody. I can speak to those things. But I didn't have any experiences of not being taken care of, not feeling loved. Not feeling like my momma was over there, my daddy was over here. What I did know early on, is although everything felt fine; it was not fine. I guess I was able to gauge that as a young person. For example, they would shuffle us to a place where they would demand we'd go and be quiet, while they argued; you could hear the aggression... And it was always about bills, or another woman or another man.*

Vee: *Can you talk about your place in your sibling order, then and now?*

Momma: *My place as a baby growing up was perfection. The only human that had a problem with me was my daddy. It was always a family running joke that my daddy didn't want to own me because I was so light. I was yellow. I was born* *extremely fair. My mother had extremely fair skin, and I was born that way. My older sister was born the exact shade of my daddy, and my older brother was born kind of a fair, caramel-colored; in the middle between momma and daddy. That was part of my trauma, because I didn't like being light. Everybody talked about me. I hated it. You gotta know, everybody was either two years or five years apart. We had the two sets of older kids, and then as I was born, that was the longest range before momma had babies again. Well, before babies actually made it. Let's say that- she lost two in between… When my younger brother was born, ironically enough, he was born looking like an inkspot. And the jokes, again, were about how light I was.*

Slavery and Jim Crow laws dictated that the "one-drop rule" suggested that one signal drop of "Black blood" makes a person Black. This idea originated from the South, becoming the universal definition for Black. This rule mattered most during slavery when deciding which of our great grands were worthy to be house-slaves cooking and sexing master, or which one of our great grands were destined to be a field slave, working outdoors in extreme heat, fingers bleeding from picking cotton, scared to disobey, and too frightened to run away. These jobs were usually determined by how dark or light the slave's skin was. Lighter women were generally house slaves. Darker women (oftentimes less valued, and considered to be unattractive) were field slaves. While this part of our history is rarely discussed in Black families, it is often played out in family dynamics. My momma experienced colorism as a child; my momma was made to feel unwanted because of the fairness of her skin. Terms like redbones, light skin, and sayings like, "you're so pretty for a dark girl" or "you look good for a dark guy" is the way Black people have been trained to stigmatize one another within our own race; it's a form of self-hatred. That, in itself, is traumatic.

Vee: *Tell me about being so young and becoming a wife to daddy. How did you manage to be someone's better half with such a disconnect happening between you and grandma at the time?*

Momma: *I was groomed to be a Stepford wife. That literally meant that we were expected to abide by the cultural "rule" that you don't let family business outside of your walls. In other words, what happens in your home, stays in your home. That's culturally true for most African-American families.*

I also taught my kids this rule; it was the only thing I knew to teach them. You gotta know, I started parenting my kids as early as 17-years-old, and I started parenting my kids in the home I shared with my mother. The disconnect happened between my mother and I when your daddy hit the scene. I was my momma's mini-me, her right hand, her perfectionist. I was the one who got everything right at school. I was cute because I was the one that looked most like her. I was outgoing. My older sister was not outgoing, she was quiet and introverted. My older brother was born a bad ass. And when I say bad ass, from the stories I was told, nobody could really control him. I was told that he was so bad that he would fall out, kick and scream. I remember several times him getting a whoopin', and him running, falling over something, and all of us ending up at the emergency room.

My momma did everything she could to separate me from your daddy, including taking my princess phone out of my room. And then when we had our first pregnancy scare, I think the realization hit her that she had lost me. I think she counted on me for the same shit I counted on you for. I was good at making everything look good. I knew when and how to respond, make the other kids respond to me. In other words, I was the administrative assistant to my momma. I would make all things right when they were wrong. But suddenly, when I got pregnant, she disconnected from me and that was foreign to me. I had never not been able to count on her; I had never been to a place where I felt like I needed resources, and she wouldn't be there to help me find them.

Typical. This is so very typical in the Black family. Oftentimes, Black pregnant teens flee from their families' homes or get kicked out of their homes. That's the reality of most of my own friends and for my own momma. So many young Black mommas felt that abandonment first from their own momma's, feeling empty on a full womb...

Interviewing my momma took a lot of guts. But I got plenty of guts.

What I don't have is an understanding of these things she recalled, because my momma made sure through my pregnancies, I never felt alone. So, I just couldn't relate. I also couldn't relate to this person she described, better known as my daddy. It's almost as if he was being reintroduced to me.

She went through a timeline that involved her living with my grandma, eventually moving out, getting an apartment, and then becoming homeless again. So, she had to live with granny and with three kids: me, my brother, and my older sister.

From there, things seemed to have gotten worse. Momma said that my daddy was at home less and less, juggling jobs and enduring the struggles of a Black man. He was also responsible for a home that his own dad had abandoned.

Then, my momma got pregnant for the fourth time. This time she gave birth to my baby sister, who was born with cerebral palsy. My momma said that at that point, she was clinically depressed. She explained that she felt even more disconnected from my daddy.

And my mom had no idea that my daddy was using drugs. She only thought he was dealing drugs. My momma said she hated living with my grandma and my grandma couldn't stand my daddy for having my momma and my siblings in such financial turmoil, landing us all back under granny's roof.

Vee: *How did you find out daddy was on crack cocaine?*

Momma: *After we got kicked out of Forest Park, we were homeless for two weeks before we moved into my momma's house. Momma bought me a pony pack. I had no idea what it was. It's like a tiny envelope, and this is how they used to serve cocaine, I guess. She brings me this pony pack, and she is the person that told me about your daddy using cocaine. I remember when she told me, we were in the living room at 4156 W. Monroe. We had gotten up that morning and I was trying to hurry and shuffle around because I always wanted to get up, get you guys cleaned up, get you breakfast so that we didn't seem like a disruption in her home. But, none of it was working. She was just irritated that we were there. Probably was thinking and saying to herself, "Look at this bastard that has knocked my daughter up four times, and is now on my living room floor." And so as I was hurrying up, trying to get you guys ready, she brought me the pony pack. She told me "Here." I had no idea what it was she was showing me. That was the day that things escalated. She kicked us out.*

We ended up walking the streets day in and day out until my brother, your uncle, came and picked us up and took us to the hotel where the neighborhood prostitutes turned tricks; It was beneath one of the restaurants that your daddy worked in. We weren't allowed to bring kids in there, so we hid you guys in the backseat of the car, really mainly trying to keep you quiet. You were the baby at the time. I felt so horrible for you not having a life with me as a newborn baby, which is probably why I pour into you so much right now. I felt like before you could actually be a baby, came a crippled younger sister. There was no time to baby you. I felt so bad about that...

This! This is the part of the interview where I lost my composure.

Tears welled up in my eyes because at that moment, I could remember feeling exactly what she was describing to me. At a very young age, I felt very alone.

Growing up, I felt extremely out of place, but necessary. Even as a child, I knew that I'd grow to understand my place in my family, and just how different it was from my siblings. Even from my parents.

So, my daddy was working three jobs at the time, because a Black man in the 90s needed that many jobs to still be poor and live in disgusting, disgraceful residences with barely any resources. Not much has changed...

Vee: *When do you begin to see your trauma bleed into us, your children?*

Momma: *Once we were finally past our homeless stage, we managed to move you all into this building and it was the absolute worst. We had maybe two folding chairs, chaise lounges. They were the really old kind. That would be our seating. We had a 13-inch television that I think my momma had given us. Essentially, we were probably between two rooms. I had four kids and rats that were probably bigger than my four kids. And I remember my son at that moment. Daddy was at work and would bring dinner home later. So, your brother put us all in the middle room, he decorated the bedroom, he took all the covers and folded them up and put them in the corner. He took the two chairs, sat them on the corner of the room. He put the TV on a milk crate, bought a little something for a table for your little sister's bootle, and he put all the old sheets and tucked them under every door in the bedroom. He said, "Don't worry momma, can't no rats get in. Imma take care of you."*

I felt so bad. I knew, right then and there, the pressures that were on my son. I remember being so upset that we had put that pressure on our child.

My momma cried during the interview. Especially while talking about the trauma my brother experienced; it is that same trauma that he fought against his whole life - until his life was snuffed out...

The next morning, Momma told me how hard it was to tell me those things and how she could barely sleep with so much of that on her mind.

I didn't dare tell her it was the same for me. But I figured she knew it anyway...

That unresolved trauma in my momma's life had come out, so vulnerably. And so much of her family's history didn't seem like history at all; It seemed new when we actually talked about it. While talking with me, my momma rediscovered all that pain that she had as a young girl. The funny thing about Black history in America is that it doesn't tell us much of what's wrong with us as Black folks, nor does history teach us who we've become because of it.

History has pretty much refused to teach the fact that there were ongoing lynchings of Black bodies and massacres between 1866 and 1920, and that these horrific murderous acts have had a major impact on Black people's psyches. As the saying goes, "hurt people, hurt people." And the first victims of that pain are usually those who are closest to you – your friends, and your family. This is the simplest explanation as to why Black families bear the brunt of dysfunction, betrayal, and self-hatred. The less simple explanation is the one that dissects the post-traumatic slave syndrome.

This term, coined by researcher Dr. Joy DeGruy, is used to describe the multigenerational trauma and injustices experienced by Black people. Her book, Post Traumatic Slave Syndrome, states:

"Although slavery has a long been a part of human history, American chattel slavery represents a case of human trauma incomparable in scope, duration, and consequence to any other incidence of human enslavement. Post-traumatic slave syndrome is a condition that exists when a population has experienced multigenerational trauma resulting from centuries of slavery and continues to experience oppression and institutionalized racism today. Added to this condition is a belief (real or imagined) that the society in which they live is not accessible to them."

In lieu of what Dr. DeGruy describes as the impact of slavery, we can be whomever we choose to be with a Facebook account and some good WiFi. Given the ridiculous amount of time we spend perusing the internet, we don't have much time remaining to confront our trauma. We do, however, have all the time and energy in the world (seemingly) to make our trauma look good. Oftentimes, we put ourselves "on display" by posting deep memes to gather "likes" so that we can appear to be more woke than the next person. If you are Black and live in Chicago, your social media timeline involves at least one R.I.P post a day. And the family dysfunction plays right out on social media as we witness the falling out of baby mommas with their baby daddies. We're more transparent and vulnerable on social media than we are with ourselves. More dedicated to making it look good externally, that we've begun to neglect the actual healing needing to happen internally. And on-screen, our enemies could look like our homies. People pleasing and "post posing" has become second nature to us. The very idea of taking our trauma public to heal ourselves and others is stuck in viral memes that only sound good, but very few of us are actually doing the real work.

Hood Healing

Sifting through trauma and being honest about its impact is just the start of the work. Doing things differently than what you saw at home, or on the streets of Chicago, is the next step. Leading the conversation on individual healing to inspire generational healing is sacred work. I'd rather do that now, than watch my children suffer from the unhealed trauma in which I inflicted on them.

Similar, yet vastly different, to the trauma in which my momma and daddy inflicted upon me. As Frederick Douglass said, "It is easier to build strong children, than to repair broken men."

Abolitionist Frederick Douglass understood the fragility of Black people. We are still fragile. Still easily broken. Easily scarred, like the backs of our brown ancestors from chains and whips being thrashed across their flesh while white slave masters shouted out Holy scriptures. Slave masters twisted the scriptures to keep our ancestors in bondage. Some of us are still in bondage...

It is difficult to heal from the truth of our past when deeply embedded in our consciousness is how ugly and worthless we are, and there is no credit given to us for the labor and sacrifices we've made for this country.

Consider that only a decade after the end of slavery, during reconstruction, a dozen, formerly owned slaves, were members of Congress. We had a Black governor: P.B.S. Pinchback, Governor of Louisiana (1872) and the first Black governor in the U.S. We knew we had the creativity, education, and cognitive ability, but it took hundreds of years of our parents being beaten to death, babies sold, and mothers raped before our brilliance was recognized. And only ten years post-slavery did we begin to see that we had these abilities. Then, enters Jim Crow. Jim Crow laws legalized racial segregation by denying Black people the right to vote, a right to an education, hold high-paying jobs, elected offices and live in white communities. Jim Crow was another method to suppress Black achievement; another tactic to divide the culture and erase the truth. Jim Crow laws sought to exclude Blacks from every sector of society.

And when we feel that exclusion, that hatred toward who we are, oftentimes we inappropriately display that pain. However, when we are brave enough to fight, we end up fighting the wrong people and displacing our anger.

We hurt our children, because our parents left us with pain to pass down. We hurt our siblings, because they are there to take our displaced hurt; we often take them for granted. We hurt our own parents, because they've caused us unapologetic and unexplainable pain, so much pain that we have trouble articulating it for ourselves. We hurt our ancestors, because we haven't learned from them; we haven't learned how to heal, something they were never allowed to do while chained to other human bodies, months at a time during the Middle Passage, witnessing their kin being sold and raped. That pain is still there and the diminishing of our ancestors' existence, the wiping away of their language, their culture, and their heritage, has yet to be a lesson for us.

We hurt ourselves and our own kin because we were taught to hate ourselves- and because we actually do.

Chapter Four

ELECTIONS, EQUITY, EMPATHY & EXCELLENCE

FEATURING SYLVIA SNOWDEN
CAN TV Producer, and Journalist

THEY **MADE** US LEARN THE **U.S. CONSTITUTION** INSIDE OF BUILDINGS NAMED AFTER **WHITE** MEN WHO **ENSLAVED** OUR **PEOPLE.**

The same constitution that reads, "all men are created equal" and something about a more perfect union. It was all a lie, and nowhere near perfect. Every line I memorized to graduate from the 8th grade was a lie. And I knew there was a reason why they were forcing that rhetoric down our throats, through our chakras. The U.S. education system fed us so many untruths. The curriculum conditioned Black children to believe that our history began in slavery instead of on the shores of Africa, FREE Africa. And now, the fight for critical race theory to be taught in schools is just another reminder of how one-sided our country's education really is.

I wrote about the closure of Chicago Public Schools (CPS) in 2011 and then again in 2020. In that decade stretch, I covered the closure of Austin High School and in 2020, the displacement of North Lawndale Community Academy.

This goes to show you how far back these issues go and how CPS is still displacing its most vulnerable populations, once again showing little to no concern about their Black lives. And it's easy to miseducate, or not educate, the population about illiteracy, docile behavior, and low self-worth. The American education system has created this façade for Black folks to presume that slavery was an unbelievably long time ago, and that we are so far removed from those vicious acts ever happening again because a change gone come. They got us hoodwinked on let freedom ring because we landed on Plymouth Rock and Plymouth Rock didn't land on us.

Hood Healing

Sure.

I found that the only journalism that mattered was the documentation that said this idea was fugazi. Fu. The truth was the only journalism I ever wanted to cover and read.

And the number one basis is this: Blacks folks in inner-city living conditions are still slaves. Surprise! I figured it out.

Run my reparations.

Except now, the inequities in our hoods have made us crippled and stagnant. It's nearly impossible to beat the odds in environments meant to beat you.

Like me, Sylvia Snowden spends her career as a broadcast journalist documenting the impact of the inequities that have a direct impact on our trauma. Sylvia is a TV show producer for Chicago Access Network Television (CAN TV), an independent, nonprofit public cable television network.

CAN TV notoriously produces stories that often go untold. These stories include, but by no means are they limited to, the disparities that exist in Black and Brown communities in Chicago.

Sylvia, too, is a Chicago kid; she grew up in Calumet Heights.

"A lot of people haven't really heard of it. It's over East and kind of made up of two different neighborhoods, Pill Hill and Stoney Island Park," Sylvia explained. "The interesting thing is that people don't think it's (Calumet Heights) the South Side. It's more like high-middle class, well-paid union workers, doctors, and lawyers."

Sylvia said that compared to how other people were living in Chicago, she and her family were living decent in a small community.

"Even though that may be where you grow up, you can't really stay," she explained. "The larger South Side is waiting."

Sylvia is the firstborn. Her parents married; her dad was an attorney, her mother a federal contractor.

Vee: *Can you describe your reality growing up in Calumet Heights?*

Sylvia: *I thought the Cosby's were real life growing up. My family was sort of like that; I thought that was everybody's reality. I didn't know for years that not* everybody lived like that. I guess after a while, we weren't really living like that, either though. My mom was diagnosed with Lou Gehrig's disease when I was in the 5th grade and died when I was a freshman in high school. That opened my eyes. Not everybody had two parents. Not too many parents took them places. But still, growing up in a situation where you wonder how you're going to eat, if the utilities are going to be on... I didn't understand that that was some people's every day. It took me to graduate from college to see how different Black folks' lives were.

Vee: *When did you realize the power in your voice?*

Sylvia: *I don't know if I realized my voice was powerful, per se. Even though I had the degree, I didn't really know if I could do it; I don't think I knew straight away that I could be a good journalist. I don't wanna say that being in journalism school made me contemplate whether or not to write. I also had this thing of I know-what-I-want-to-do-but-I-don't-really know-if-I-could-get-in-that-lane. I knew I wanted to tell stories, but I didn't know if there was a niche for the type of stories I wanted to tell, in the way I wanted to tell them. When I first got out there, I just didn't know.*

Sylvia graduated from the University of Missouri and then began an internship at WVON Radio 1690, Chicago's Urban Legacy Station.

Vee: *How has storytelling changed you?*

Sylvia: *I think, if I'm being 100% honest, there was a part of me that got into journalism for my ego; To see my name in print, in lights, and for my own purposes, my own selfish purposes, frankly. And what ended up happening, what I've found is that there are a lot of*

Black people on the South Side who have these stories that people never ever get to hear. There are stories that never get to be told, that I now have the power to tell. I could tell stories, and I found there was power in that. I think at that point, it turned from a career into a calling. There are people's stories that truly need to be told. When that became my mindset, I saw a shift.

Vee: *Did you understand other people's perspectives about Chicago and the South Side?*

Sylvia: *I didn't understand the way everybody viewed the South Side. I didn't understand that everybody thought it was just badlands full of criminal Black people who just walk around killing each other all day – I didn't have this*

Hood Healing

understanding. I also didn't understand some of the struggles that our own people have. And not only do you not understand that these are real people living real lives, but you also fail to understand the trauma that people have gone through. While you think they are doing poorly in life, if you knew some of their stories, you would commend them. But when you don't have exposure, it is difficult for you to be able to treat their stories fairly and do the stories justice.

Vee: *Can you talk to me about a time that you experienced trauma? How did it change you?*

Sylvia: *My upbringing made me believe in Black excellence. I heard that phrase all the time growing up. My parents were very intentional. I had a Black principal in elementary school, my doctor was Black, my dentist was Black. These were all Black people, telling me I was smart and that they expected great things of me.*

I remember working with a second-grader. Her dad was in jail and her mom was trying to raise her and her other siblings. Her teacher came to me and told me she was failing math; she couldn't add or subtract. I remember helping her with this addition worksheet and seeing her struggle with adding in the second grade. I remember going to her mother and saying 'She's really struggling with this and if she can't figure it out, she isn't going to third grade.' Her mother looked at me and said 'I'm so glad you can help her. She asked me, and I didn't know how.'

Some people judge young Black kids and how they perform in school academically. I couldn't imagine being 8 years old and not being able to go to my mom for help with my homework. But when you judge people based upon your experiences, instead of their experiences, it's easy for you to dismiss them as not motivated, or dumb, or lazy. I had to understand that, especially before I could really understand trauma and how to tell the stories of the traumatized. There are people that don't even have a lens.

Sylvia knows a thing or five about the Chicago trauma. Like Garrard and I, she mourns a member of her family from the bloody boulevards. She even wrote about it.

"It was Saturday, January 2, 2016, when I got the call about 7:00 a.m. that my cousin Ricky had been shot to death while sitting in his car," Sylvia shared. "Normally, I'd leave my phone right next to me at night. I kept seeing the flashing light of the phone, thinking I was having a dream. He wasn't just murdered. Executed, frankly. He was shot 13 times in the face, neck, chest, and ear," Sylvia explained. *"I don't wish that on anybody, even the people I don't like. If you never had that happen to you, it's difficult to really understand or to know what that feels like."*

However, the trauma continued after Ricky was murdered.

Vee: *What do you immediately remember after experiencing the trauma of receiving a call that your cousin, Ricky, was murdered?*

Sylvia: *We were trying to process as a family what had happened; we hadn't had a death in the family since 1992. In addition to processing the trauma of what happened to him, I ended up having the additional trauma of going online trying to figure out who could have done this to him. We didn't know anything. I remember reading the small blurbs on the local news outlets saying somebody was killed, on New Year's night; the third murder in the city that year, at about 10:00 at night. And oh, the police said he was a documented gang member.*

Talk about adding insult to injury... At that moment, something in me snapped. I thought to myself, what is wrong with these people? I held on to that anger for like a year. I kept thinking about all these young people that lost their lives this way - Trayvon Martin, Mike Brown... and something in me just snapped!

Fueled by her cousin Ricky's murder, Sylvia wrote a story titled "They Called My Dead Cousin A 'Gang Member'" that got republished by *HuffPost* (Feb. 2017), formerly known as *Huffington Post*, that went viral.

Vee: *How did your article change the trajectory of your journalism? And how did your cousin's murder impact that?*

Sylvia: *What I said in the article was that my cousin was murdered, and that that was bad enough. But imagine being a relative of somebody who was killed so viciously and having to go online and see him described to a city of three million people (and most of them didn't even know him) as a documented gang member. I said in my article that is a code; it is a racially tinged code used all the time for young Black people to suggest that they die violent deaths, and somehow cause their own deaths. They did it to Trayvon Martin, suggesting that somehow smoking marijuana in high school made him a bad kid that caused his own death.*

I want to be fair and clear: Our family doesn't have any misgivings about the bad things Ricky may have been into. He had some difficulties as a kid and as a young man. He had been in and out of trouble; he had been to jail. I'm not going to say he didn't have challenges. But the person who died that day was a husband and a father of six who was raising his children. He had a job he was getting up and going to every day. For the people who work for these news stations, who don't know him, to disrespect him like that...He can't defend himself. He's dead. It was too much. But it's not just my cousin. It happens to all of these other young people -Trayvon, Mike Brown...they weren't perfect kids. But why do Black kids have to be perfect before we're sorry that they're dead? Why should Black parents have to go on TV and convince you of what a good kid they had? What about the fact that this was a young person, who had their whole lives in front of them, and now they're gone?

It's a challenge to reach excellence when day-to-day life is discouraging. Young, Black people begin to emulate behaviors of rap artists, NBA players, and actors, never believing so much in reaching the so-called American Dream. Due to the lack of positive Black male role models in the hood, including dads, and due to the lack of male mentoring programs in the hood, Black boys in Chicago aspire for a life more like G Herbo, and less like the low-key family man working a 9 to 5. In Chicago, where the unemployment rates are currently over 7%, there is more motivation for a young, Black man to stand outside of Maxwell's on Independence Blvd. and sell his product to crack fiends. In most cases, making his momma dread that call, like the one my momma received for my brother.

Recent studies show that there are now more Black women graduating college than any other race in the United States. Studies showed us that in 2019, nearly 10% of Black women earned a college degree. These days, women make up 57% of college students, outnumbering the number of Black men in college. Yet, Black women still struggle to obtain equal pay and treatment at their jobs.

According to the U.S. Census, on average, Black women were paid 63% of white men's salaries in that same year, 2019. To break this down further, it would take a Black woman 19 months to make what a white man can make at the same job in just 12 months.

And that's bogus as hell.

Yet, the whole world seems to taunt, haunt, hate, terrorize and disrespect the Black woman.

The history I know says that Black women are the center of the Earth and that life started within, and with, a Black woman. It was the Black woman who was the homemaker, cleaner, cooker, seamstress, sex slave, and ego stroker for the white slave masters. It was the breastmilk of my great, great, great grandmothers that nursed the babies that are now making more money than me and my Black counterparts.

And now, more and more Black women are leaving the daycare industry due to lack of pay. According to PBS, 20% of the daycare industry nationwide has lost workers. Most workers across the country said they are leaving the industry due to burnout. About 97% of early educators are women, and of those women, 40% are either Black, Brown or immigrant women.

Women all over the United States and in other countries like China, Russia, Sudan are vanishing, and in some cases, dying. The Black bodies of mothers, daughters, sisters are being sex trafficked, snatched up, raped, killed, criticized for having abortions, criticized for having too many kids or too many baby daddies. Black bodies are being used to advance medical science. Society judges the Black woman for being too independent, and for being "lazy" if you're collecting SNAP benefits and WIC. Black women... Sandra Bland, Sojourner Truth, Henrietta Lacks...

The pain carried in our hips travels up our spines, making it harder to carry on our backs. That pain is as heavy as the babies on our hearts that we birthed into the world that hates us and hates the little boys that become the men that are endlessly murdered without remorse and for the simple crime of being caught Black in the wrong place at the wrong time.

With all the Black woman is to the Universe, the Black woman oftentimes feel like NOTHING.

As Black people, at the deepest core of our beings, we were conditioned to believe that we simply weren't enough. This is a barrier that prevents our hearts from healing.

Let's travel back down those bloody boulevards, though. The same streets that took my brother, took Garrard's parents and Sylvia's cousin. The local media would be all over the details of the killings, but never many details on why these things were happening – besides the quintessential "gang affiliation" headline. So much of the murders in Black communities were direct results of the inequities displayed toward Blacks. In addition to education, housing inequalities impact our families. Redlining, which dates back to the 1930s, created the obstacles of allowing Black people to receive home loans, most inner-city families had become accustomed to apartment living, or shared space.

Hood Healing

I remember living in Austin and our cousins lived right above us. At that time, we thought that was the best setup. I mean, it was better than the project buildings my other cousins were growing up in. Project living in Chicago resulted in Black people, once again, being forced to survive in spaces that were unfit, unsanitary, dirty, and destitute. Projects were high-rise slave ships, with windows and concrete walls. The housing inequities over time became compounded with the food inequities which led to obesity, hypertension, and cancers. Death was close to us by way of unhealthy conditions. Death was close to us by way of our homes. Death was close to us by way of our families and friends. Black people in Chicago often have trouble finding a win in situations when the odds are overwhelmingly stacked against them.

Discomfort outside the home creates disarray inside of the walls of Black homes in Chicago. Disassociation of this disarray plays out in our own friendships and intimate relationships, oftentimes resulting in physical fights, police sirens, and the baby daddy getting arrested. I am not an exception to this "rule." In my case, he and I both got arrested. More than once.

I knew I was traumatized when I found myself next to a bloody man (my eldest daughter's dad) behind his garage and scared for the cops to come. I had scratched him up pretty bad this time. And the time before that, too. I knew then that my life was at its lowest. I was my absolute sickest...yet, living in this perfect, pretend universe that I had created.

Yet...it wasn't pretending. I really did live a perfect life...at least as far as the eye could see. However, I was stuck in two worlds. In one world, I was an abuser, provoking fights in a premature relationship with little- to-no understanding of why. In the other world, I was a stable mother. A college graduate. A published writer. A community leader.

Everyone adored me. But, I hated myself.

That abusive life landed me at 1500 Maybrook Drive in Maywood, IL. That's the Illinois Circuit Court of Cook County in Maywood. This was right near my hometown, Bellwood, which later became the place where I eventually stood before a judge explaining why I deserved to keep custody of my firstborn because I showed signs of being an abusive parent. A criminal record with years of domestic abuse charges and documented anger issues made it even easier for a judge to believe that I was abusive.

I was still a good mom, though.

The judge disagreed.

"Do you have any last words, Ms. Harrison?", the judge had asked me after I had lost the custody battle, and the courts decided that I wasn't a fit mother. Imagine that. A college graduate, well-spoken, carried myself well, but angry, and abusive. And even worse, unclear of my behaviors.

Why was fighting such a big deal? I had grown up with people bickering and brawling outside out west all the time. It was normal. Or, at least I thought it was. Hitting someone after they upset you, or doing something upsetting to you, was how afterwards things were handled around me growing up. School fights where crowds of people gathered to see somebody get whooped. Trauma on the school playground- smh...

What I knew is that when I got into trouble, I got a whoopin. My momma got whoopins. Her momma got whoopins. Slavery taught our culture an act that had become so normal, so necessary to survival. The traumatic way of handling one another's bodies, one another's feelings, had become ingrained in our culture.

I whooped my daughter, in the way in which I had learned to discipline. Out of anger. And to make a point. And to control her behavior. Just as the slave master did.

Well, the judge made a point with me. Gave me a child support order and all. And a distant child who was never to reside in my home for her entire childhood.

Healing from that feels impossible. It's a humiliation I wear daily. Humiliation you wouldn't see on Facebook or Instagram.

The stressors and depressions of our home-life entice us to self-medicate. The deep desire for weed, liquor, and other substances to numb and neglect the depths of our sadness is why Black inner-city neighborhoods have more liquor stores than grocery stores. Chicago's hypes are getting high before sunrise. Searching spaces on the ground's concrete for their next numbing dose.

Dr. Sorrell explained to me that using drugs is a coping mechanism, especially for youth, and is oftentimes generational. Drug abuse is usually a direct result of someone experiencing trauma, a way of looking to numb themselves from pain.

"Unfortunately, a substance is easier to get a hold of than a therapist," explained Dr. Sorrell.

Hood Healing

Dr. Sorrell also shared that one of the biggest issues in mental health right now is being able to place and provide youth mental health services. She explained that in some cases, young people in

Chicago and other parts of the world can be added to a waiting list of a month or longer, despite an immediate crisis.

"Particularly in Chicago, we have children that may wait in emergency room beds for two weeks, maybe three weeks, before being transferred to a mental health facility and services that they may need."

In 2012, former Mayor Rahm Emanuel shut down 50% of the city's mental health care facilities. Studies show that more than half of the city's population is suffering from mental health issues, especially in the last past year as the city faced a pandemic. Community violence spiraled out of control and folks' finances had fallen off tremendously. Last year, 2020, was an especially telling year for Black folks in Chicago. While the world suffered the effects of a worldwide pandemic that killed over 20,000 people, Black folks suffered greater because the pandemic disproportionately affected our communities. Underlying conditions were just code for Black folks without good health. And hypertension, obesity, and diabetes. It was harder to fight against a pandemic with all that going on. On top of already not having good food options in the hood, the hood also didn't have good healthcare options. Black people in inner-city Chicago were out there bad, before the pandemic.

I hit the city's scene in '87. That's exactly six years after President Ronald Reagan originally took office and successfully sold the American people the War on Drugs; a conversation that really should have been documented as the War on Black people, since this supposed War on Drugs landed so many of our dads, brothers, uncles and sons in prison. Prison was just the newly developed slavery by the time I was born.

Harold Washington had made history as Chicago's first Black Mayor four years prior, and Chicago had issued record rainfall and floods in August of 1987. More than nine inches of rain fell in less than one day.

And most times in Chicago, when it rains, it pours.

Chapter Five

GENERATIONS, GDS, GRIEF & GROWTH

FEATURING NA-TAE' THOMPSON
Co-Founder of True Star Foundation

CITY STORMS POURED RIGHT INTO 2020. CHICAGO GETTING HIT BY COVID-19 WAS ALL BAD.

Media outlets reported that Chicago was among several other hotspot cities for rising COVID cases - Detroit, Indiana, and Baltimore...all predominantly Black inner-cities. Reportings on these things from the areas in which I grew up was sad as hell. Black folks in Chicago were dropping like flies because pre-existing health conditions (i.e. Diabetes, high blood pressure) only added to the spread of the pandemic. Remote learning was mandated and young people were forced out of school where many of them felt safer than being at home. Two, sometimes three generations of Black and Brown people under one roof made it hard to control the spread of COVID.

On the West and South sides of Chicago, residents seeing suffering in that way were triggered. Black people were often the last to receive medical treatment at inner-city hospitals and were left to die unattended in overcrowded hospital hallways. We lost masses of Black people during the first months of the pandemic. Then, word of a newly created vaccine began to circulate in the hood. Black people were hesitant to receive it- and with good reason. The history of the United States using Black folks to experiment with unethical medical treatment and research began to resurface. Case and point: the Tuskegee Study of Untreated Syphilis in 1932 and 1972 by the U.S. Public Health Service and the Centers for Disease Control and Prevention where Black people were used as guinea pigs to observe the natural history of untreated syphilis in Black populations. The Black men who participated in this study during that time were unaware of what was happening and were lied to. So, now, Black folks shy away from vaccinations that once claimed to save Black lives -- but actually killed Black people.

During the pandemic, Black people in Chicago's inner-city neighborhoods

Hood Healing

were also reminded that good healthcare belonged to people above their income grade and that local hospitals in Chicago like Loretto and St. Anthony barely had equipment and staff for the COVID patients that walked through their doors. So, to be able to accommodate a pandemic wasn't realistic.

What is realistic, however, is the 336 homicides in Chicago so far this year. And before this book goes to print, that number will increase. Perhaps even double. Chicago's violence has made national news. The city has dubbed nicknames like Chiraq and was titled the murder capital of the nation in 2018.

Chicago has also made headlines recently because of its opioid crisis, COVID cases, and political scandals. As a journalist, a mother, and a Black woman, I started to wonder if it was something about Chicago. Or something about the people in Chicago...

After some reading and writing, and more understanding, I realized it was both the city's culture and the slave culture that was intertwining.

Dr. Sorrell explained that Black people typically have unresolved grief.

"We have such unresolved grief. When we express grief, it may not just be for a loved one we've lost, but all of the other potential loved ones lost. We have collective grief for several areas where we've experienced loss. Our grief, as well as our joy, screams from such inner-wellings of not being able to either express, to process, or to be able to have as a process where you move forward and the grief fully melts with time."

Due to the ongoing violence in our communities, young, Black people in Chicago face grief daily; it's toxic. As Dr. Sorrell mentioned, our grief is unresolved because the violence is never-ending and we don't have the mental and emotional capacity, nor the resources to process the multitude of traumas we've experienced. Mental health clinics are scarce, positive role models are usually on TV, and enrichment programs to support the visions of young people are hard to find.

"The common thread with young people in Chicago is their desire to want more, want better, and to be successful, but many of them don't know how," said Na-Tae' Thompson, Co-Founder and Executive Director of True Star Foundation and True Star Media. True Star is a Chicago-based, multimedia organization for middle school and high school aspiring journalists and communications professionals. They promote news literacy and prepare

young people in Chicago's neighborhoods for the workforce through summer and afterschool apprenticeships.

I brought in Na-Tae' to help paint the picture of Chicago's youth and the challenges they face. And she also had some solutions to offer.

Vee: *What typically hinders the growth potential of our Chicago youth?*

Na-Tae': *With the young people that are challenged with exposure, I would definitely say their household is the challenge. If the parents don't know certain things about day-to-day life, the kids definitely aren't going to know. If you have a parent or guardian and all they know is Englewood, for example, they're not going to leave Englewood. And this is generational. That lack of exposure and knowledge is just going to keep getting passed on.*

So, when you have a young person that comes to True Star programs, and you find yourself frustrated and upset because they lack knowledge, hit the pause button. They just don't know. They are children. If they don't have that exposure and knowledge from home, you can't fault them. We try to expand their world and knowledge base; expose them to certain things to provide them with a different experience. It's about your background and what you have exposure to at home and outside of school. You have some kids that may want to go to Whitney Young, for example, and they've signed themselves up to take the test, they've driven themselves to take the test, yet they may not have that parental support, but they want more. It's a mixture of young people in Chicago, but at the end of the day, they all want the same thing: they want to be happy.

Happiness, however, is hard to come by when the majority of Black youth in the city are mourning the loss of their friends. Headlines this past July read that four shootings in Chicago left three dead, including a teenager. Weeks later on July 9, a Northbrook teen was shot and killed while visiting family in Chicago.

In Chicago, the endless and senseless killings of the sons of Black mommas are as common as the Chicago Police Department not solving homicides. It's too common. The *True Star Foundation* didn't just provide any ole common solution for the issue of youth violence in the city and getting them out of harm's way. *True Star* knew that our Chicago youth needed jobs and money. *True Star* provided the motivation for youth to join an apprenticeship program across the city, get paid and stay off the streets.

Vee: *How do youth programming and workforce development intersect with community violence?*

Na-Tae': *When you do a program like True Star, anything after school in those high-crime peak hours, between about 3:00 p.m. and 6:00 p.m., is potentially life-saving. We are trying to combat the disturbing content they are consuming, by teaching them to control their own narrative and be content creators. We have students who are already on track to be great. But then we have students who are right on the border, their lives could go either way. Then we have students that have absolutely no idea what they want to do and just participate in the program because they know that at the close of the program they'll get paid a check. Either way, the time that they participate in the program means that they are not a victim or perpetrator of violence during those peak hours. In Chicago, It doesn't matter what neighborhood you're in, violence can occur on any side of the city; violence knows no boundaries in Chicago anymore.*

Vee: *Where would the city be if we didn't have youth programs and mentors pouring into the youth?*

Na-Tae': *I think the city would be worse off. While you won't capture every young person, you're going to get some. And if we don't have these types of programs, that means no one is getting captured and is left to the vulnerability of the streets. Programs like True Star are very important to help young people try to figure it all out.*

Na-Tae' shared that there are, however, some students who are not struggling to figure it out; she explained that there are some young people in True Star programs who are from seemingly stable families with great access to resources and future wealth. Na-Tae' called those particular families, "legacy families."

Until our interview, I had never realized that the Harrisons, the family I grew up in, is a "legacy family." Like Evan and his family, we were the Huxtables on the block. The neighborhood kids came over for dinner, spent the night at our home, and called our momma "momma". As I mentioned at the beginning, my momma was a pro at masking our internal pain, so much so that we may have looked like a legacy family, acted like a legacy family ... but inside of our home, we were isolated and broken.

That's still the case.

The grief from the murder of my brother caused a different type of vibe with my entire family. Things during the week of the funeral felt extremely close. And once we closed that casket on my brother, the distance within my family that already existed only became greater.

That's what happens in Black families, more often than not. The pain of grief and how to handle it is just another thing for Black families to carry on their backs. The insulting part of all of this is the lack of respect that we receive alive, grieving, or even dead. Similar to Sylvia and her first-ever viral story, the lack of empathy in Chicago regarding the great wide-spread grief endured by Black people is barely ever acknowledged. The police don't solve the crimes and the public becomes numb to it. It's almost as if it's all normal day-to-day living: dying that is. The pain inside of some of these young people's homes often results in them looking for acceptance, outside of the home. Gangs become family. And in Chicago, gangs are usually the scapegoat to all that's wrong with the hood...

Someone got murdered? Must've been gang-affiliated.

Had to have been the Moes who shot up the block.

A Chicago cop got shot? Must've been foe n' nem.

Looting? Gotta be the GDs or Vice Lords at fault.

The gang culture in Chicago got a bad rep. Groups (gangs) that started out as outlets for community resources and community empowerment, were later painted as violent and animalistic savages. But from the ashes of some of the 90s street gangs come some sons of drug lords and daughters of insecure men who leave them before the age of two. Then later, the daughters become mothers themselves-teenage mothers, sometimes. This is the norm in Chicago where just last year the teen birth rate was higher than the national average of 18.8 births per 1,000 women between the ages of 15 and 19.

I, however, gave birth at 21. Insecure as hell. Not ready to be someone's momma nor someone's wife. I wore my trauma on my sleeve. My firstborn is the product of all that I've lived through, my lies to myself, times when I was flat-out broke and dinner was hotdogs with no buns, no ketchup either. Nights, when I was holed up in a hotel room battling suicidal thoughts after fights with my daughter's dad; she was all I had to live for...

Hood Healing

If anything, I just want to heal myself, for her.

And in case you didn't know, in my 20s I was an honor student in college from a two-parent family home. I always had a car; my daddy sold them for a living. Always clean and fed. But my inner-child cried out a lot for help that my family made sure didn't show up in public. I know my momma felt that... My inner-child cries out now for the things I've seen and can't unsee. Or unfeel. Like the feelings I caught watching my momma intimately hang with my brother's best friend, enjoying the company of him as I would normally watch her enjoy my dad's...but happier, freer. I felt the humiliation of everyone on my block knowing, and the hypocrisy of still staging ourselves as the "Huxtables" pissed me off. I spoke up about it a lot; I ignored the idea of staying in a "child's place."

My innocence was fierce because I never once was confused by the trauma I saw; I always knew exactly what my eyes were seeing... I just didn't know why and I couldn't put a name on it. Like the family molestation I witnessed that may not have included my body, but was all-inclusive to my soul. That scene forced me to understand that staying in a child's place meant I was really an active, functioning adult, seeing grown things, but had to keep quiet about them. I literally felt the impact of these things inside of myself. And some of them hurt deep, separated me from siblings, and made life extremely cloudy. Call me the oddball, the black sheep, the loner...label it what you want. I have memories of uncles that have gone away, and not off to war, but spent years in prison for things nobody really talked about. The stories I've heard at my momma's dining room table while gossiping with my auntie about family business also robbed my innocence. How uncle so and so sexually abused his women. How cousin so and so was taunted about numerous abortions. I had to listen, again, and stay in a child's place. Hearing so many of these conversations made me a storyteller at an early age. That was the good news. Yet, I had to keep these stories locked inside of me. That was the bad news. You know there is a quote that says, *"You're as sick as your secrets..."* Trauma is real.

I was a child that carried heavy family weights. I wanted to help momma make it all look good. And with that, came making sure she was okay. I've carried her burdens in my sleep and in the dreams that she was too tired to meet me in. The weight of her pain grabs at me because I know it's deeply rooted; I know it's the pains of her own mother that she carries.

Like most of us.

So, I was numb. Like most of us.

So often, in Chicago, we become numb to a vicious environment. Black people battle generations of pain and the outcry for help oftentimes goes ignored by city officials.

It's a challenge to understand your own trauma in an environment that continues to sweep your pain under rugs of political scandals, systemic garbage, and bogus laws.

It's hard to heal in a hood that hurts you.

It's easy, though, to become trapped in trap houses and cornered on corners, with no way out.

"There are, unfortunately, youth that don't have the resources needed for survival in this city," Na-Tae' said. *"We don't want young people stuck in a box, but most of them are..."*

While covering Chicago stories and living in a lowkey suburb tucked away with my babies, I always knew that folks would say I have no right to cover the hood. Some may say that writing this book from my suburban townhome is oxymoronic. And perhaps being ten years removed from a Cook County zip code doesn't qualify me to speak on inner-city blues. For me, the answer was always simple. You can take the girl out of the hood, but you can never take the hood out of the girl. I don't want to die out there. And I don't want to close a casket on a child, like my momma had to do.

And of course, because I talk now so much about healing, I must be healed, right? Because I know what it takes. Crown me the guru of healing. Nah, I have no idea what it takes! Most times. Usually, I'm alone. That's because part of my healing is healing from toxic people, who've hurt me in such a deep way, that alone feels better than forgiveness. Alone...because I, too, have hurt most people who love me. That is exactly what carrying unhealed trauma does to you. You've heard the quote, seen the meme: hurt people, hurt people. I've been hurt so many times, so I've definitely inflicted that hurt onto others.

The question becomes this: How can we stop spreading the trauma? How can we stop inflicting the same pains that have damaged us and our self-esteem, our self-worth and rebuild and restore our children, our friends, and our own communities?

Hood Healing

This is going to undoubtedly take an entire movement. Not the kind that requires us to break into the Apple Store or Louis Vuitton on Michigan Avenue. And I'm not suggesting the type of movement that sets CPD SUVs on fire, causing the mayor to issue a citywide curfew.

A lit movement, but not that kind of lit.

Black people in Chicago first need the necessary knowledge and understanding to pull off an efficient movement that will communicate to local officials to prioritize Black lives. For real this time.

We don't want any more murals or Black Lives Matter written on sidewalks or city officials wearing African prints during a Juneteenth press conference.

The knowledge of our history and the pains from our ancestors is what should motivate us to act, not just talk. It's time to flip the script on narratives that label inner-city Black folks as barbaric and uneducated. It's time to challenge our own friends and family to start spreading the idea of healing from this trauma by talking about it and being about healing it. We need to stop negatively talking about each other, and work diligently toward solutions to help one another achieve better health, housing, and hope.

We need city officials to appropriate funding in Black and Brown communities, not just recycle the same annual budgets, allocating the same funds to the same organizations. We need funding with fundamental planning, not just gentrified, modern apartment buildings with upgraded windows for more random bullets to fly through.

Chicago officials need to work toward understanding and empathizing with what Black residents feel about their living spaces, which are oftentimes not accommodating, clean or safe. We need city officials at the table who are connecting our inner-city living spaces to plantations, so that the connection is clear: the majority of Blacks and Browns in this city are living in conditions worse than stray dogs. We need city officials at the table who are making it clear that in our Chicago schools, public, private, lottery, Montessori, or whatever, we must teach critical race theory in order to connect our youth to our history. So that way, as Maya Angelou said, "When we know better, then we do better."

I ask all living generations to consider what could actually happen if we did something different with our trauma. If we allowed it to fuel us as much as we allowed it to piss us off, I wonder what we could collectively heal.

The primary solution to most problems is education. Chicago's schools need resources, qualified staff that don't appear in headlines about district scandals. We need our mayor and her entire team to understand that police do not belong in school buildings. Ever. We need to reshape the narrative around CPD and Black people's fears of the police. Black people don't feel protected in their neighborhoods where cops neglect their lives, threaten their lives, and take their lives.

In order to do this, Black folks in Chicago need to know the things that they don't know; educate themselves. What I've come to realize while reporting and writing about this city is that lack is normal to Black Chicagoans. The idea of outdated CPS buildings and the lack of grocery stores becomes a lifestyle. And so the city, state, and federal government play right into the lifestyle that is damaging our culture.

Black people need allies in Chicago. It's time for anyone in this city to stop thinking that Black people can dig our culture out of centuries of pain, alone. Racism isn't going to cease with religious and political groups constantly living by those privileged principles, pushing an agenda that isn't solving anything. Let racism go. To save the Black race, we need the human race.

After we overcome this idea that the white man is in our way, and the white culture is the one we hate, we begin to heal. We heal from the parallel pains inflicted on our ancestors. Racism breathes because our society gives it oxygen. It's time to pull the plug. Empowering the Black culture does not mean hating other cultures. With empowerment, Blacks in Chicago can become allies with other races to build Black-owned businesses and inspire Black education in our schools.

We won't all get along, like Martin Payne always wanted. We won't always see the content of one another's characters, like Martin Luther King Jr. desired. However, we will begin to move toward a future in this city where Black children grow up feeling wanted, and loved, because it isn't a part of the culture that hates them, refuses to hire them, or shoot them dead in their neighborhoods.

It came to me one moment while deep in pain over my own life, that my entire generation is grieving its ancestors. And so is my parents' generation. Grieving what they know happened either on a plantation long before their own birth or on Superbowl Sunday in an alley on Chicago's West Side. The grief is so heavy on us, so unreal to even fathom, that we don't even know what to call it.

It's trauma.

Trauma is a deeply disturbing and distressful event in your life that leaves a long-lasting impact on your life. And left untreated, trauma is toxic; it will slowly kill you.

But if you're Black, you wake up and go to bed with trauma. In Chicago, most people are completely disconnected from local news, because of its traumatic nature. Constant reports of people being murdered is literally triggering our moods in this city. No wonder everyone is on edge, no wonder people seem to be so mad. Jealous. Unsupportive. Backstabbing one another, including their own family members.

It's no wonder that for some people seemingly the best way to express anger most times is to just kill someone. That's what happened to a slave that pissed off his white master. Talked back. Didn't comply. Dead.

It's always the narrative that Black people are so angry. So wild. Always some rhetoric about Black women being promiscuous twerkers with low self-esteem and low class.

Never the narrative that the centuries of being repeatedly raped has resulted in baby after baby.

It's grown old. All the racism and hate that spreads throughout life, it's old. It's the problem, not the solution. The power invested in hating a single race so much, lying so much... These acts have proven to be detrimental to our culture.

And I'm calling it out. The problem isn't just white, rich, elite, suburban people. Often, the problem is Black people, too.

Black people in Chicago are so traumatized that we are legit calling it, "living our best lives".

And yes, some people are truly making livable wages, have nice homes and cars. Those things don't mean nothing, though, to a hurting soul that hasn't escaped a sad and dark childhood. I've watched so many people, particularly in my own family, bury every part of themselves under a vice.

It is time for action; it's time to raise the bar beyond unmeaningful memes and Netflix documentaries.

IT IS TIME TO DO SOMETHING!

If we refuse to collectively do something about the trauma inside of ourselves, it will continue to play out in our communities. We will constantly see upticks in shootings, carjackings, home invasions, credit card cracking, fraud, all that.

It is time to stop just saying it is time. Putting these needs in document form, with real stories to back up the needs, is Hood Healing.

Creating platforms for those who are right now helping shape the Black narrative of Black lives in this city, across the world, is Hood Healing.

The idea of potentially embarrassing myself, opening up my life to worldwide criticism, and not giving a damn, is Hood Healing.

The idea of revealing my own trauma, to arrive at the root of my generation's trauma, is Hood Healing.

Sacrificing my pride, for my legacy, is Hood Healing.

Understanding my place, all the way from my momma's womb, through the umbilical cord of life that connected me to her, my grandma, and her momma, is Hood Healing.

To understand the strength of my culture, and Black Power as it relates to the sun's rays and the blades of grass that are truly our ancestors being pushed by the wind, is Hood Healing.

Connecting my ancestors to my trauma and realizing that the centuries of grief deserves therapy, self-care, and love, is Hood Healing.

And giving this energy to Black lives in the hood, the necessary energy to rise up from our ancestral ashes and heal the wounds that hinder us from truly living our best lives, is Hood Healing.

Heal with me.

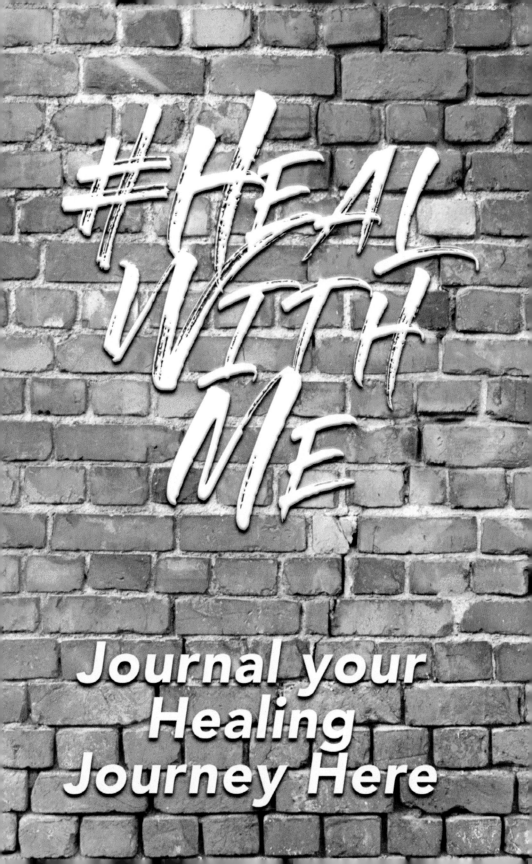

#HealWithMe

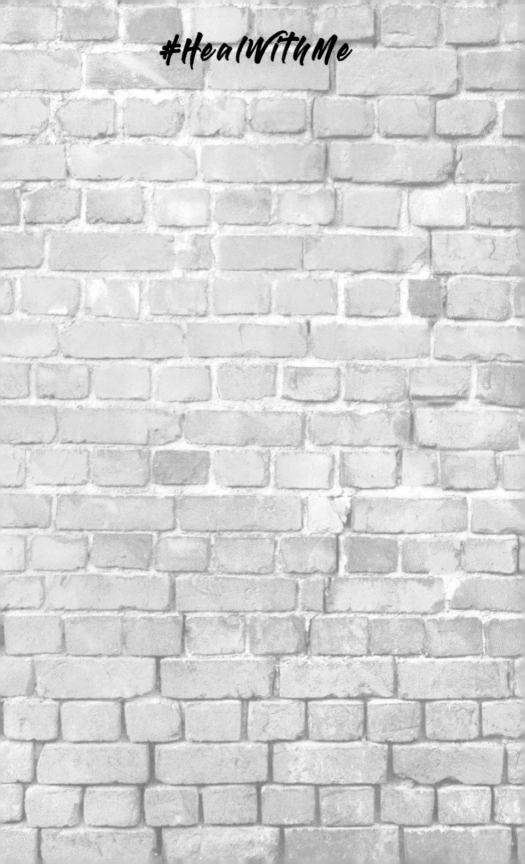
#HealWithMe

#HealWithMe

#HealWithMe

#HealWithMe

Epilogue

DISCLAIMER:

I DISCLAIM ABSOLUTELY
NOTHING.

I'm unapologetically standing on every word and revealing every uncomfortable truth and pain that just may trigger some intellectual, solution-based conversations about the need for Black people in Chicago to unpack our trauma and begin the journey of healing.

Everything has to be said so gently these days; everyone has to be accommodated so fairly. Hurting somebody's feelings to heal our lineage is a risk worth taking.

Copies sold are less important than conversations happening at tables that can shift the economic climate of the West and South sides of Chicago. I need this conversation flowing from the mouths of Black people who can move the conversation from the South Side to South Africa to aid Black babies born to be brilliant. I need this conversation to round up white shirts in corporate places owned by Black people, ready to donate time and dollars to disenfranchised schools and mental health facilities.

We are no longer waiting for a city official to promise us the bare minimum, and not even come through with that. It's either time or it's not. It's either about us or not.

We are no longer waiting for a white person in a suit to tell us what our hood needs. National media who've never crossed the 290 cannot tell us what our city needs and why we grieve.

Time to round up a crew of like-minded individuals, formerly attempted by Huey P. Newton, to talk the talk and strengthen our neighborhoods. We could be stronger now, smarter now. We've got the blood of Harriet, the knowledge of Malcolm, Marcus Garvey, Sojourner, and all her truth.

Hood Healing

The living conditions of our inner-city Chicago youth should not make anyone question why the majority of them prefer to be high, numb. They cuss like sailors and have no filters because they have no value on their lives. And they feel trapped in a city that paints its gentrified condos with Black boys' blood.

Elders are shaking their heads at generations that have come before them. Disgusted with our music videos. Disturbed by the way we, the youngsters, raise our kids and ashamed for making it all so. Escaping the accountability of why we hate our reflection, and the world they thrust us into, sometimes before 18, continuing the pattern of generational collapse.

It isn't the fault of Black people, but Black people are often to blame. The psychological implications of being tricked by our own trauma is devastating.

Revolutions kickoff with plans, gatherings, understandings. Documentation of honest Black history is our guide. This book will one day be an example of these times — a documentation of a collection of painful stories, dates, photos, and truth.

Sharing myself in this way is worth what's next.

Somebody had to do it.

As Cassius Clay (aka Muhammad Ali) once said...

I Shook Up the World!

Contributors

Dometi Pongo

Dometi Pongo is an award-winning journalist and MTV News host and correspondent, most recently for *True Life Crime* on MTV. He has also led red carpet interviews for MTV News at events like the MTV Video Music Awards (VMA's); hosted the "Conversations in Context" series on the Smithsonian Channel with Lonnie G. Bunch III, and been a news anchor for WGN Radio AM 720 and WVON 1690 AM.

Garrard McClendon

Garrard McClendon is an associate professor of education policy at Chicago State University. He holds a Ph.D. from Loyola University and has earned an Emmy Award, Associated Press Broadcasters Award, and an NAACP Champion Award. McClendon is Executive Director of the McClendon Scholarship Fund, and board member of the Sheila A. Doyle Foundation, Mid America Club, and the National Association of Wabash Men. He is the author of *Donda's Rules, President Thug, and Ax or Ask?* and is the director of the non-violence film, "Forgiving Cain." McClendon lives in Chicago.

Evan F. Moore

Evan F. Moore is a *Chicago Sun-Times* culture and entertainment reporter and the co-author of *Game Misconduct: Hockey's Toxic Culture and How to Fix It.* His work has appeared in *Rolling Stone, Bleacher Report, The Nation, Chicago Magazine, Ebony Magazine,* amongst many other publications. He is currently a freelancer for local and national media outlets and was an adjunct instructor for a news reporting class at DePaul University. Moore was recently named Press Secretary for Chicago Public Schools.

Sandra Harrison

Sandra Harrison, M.A. TRDV, is the CEO of DVA Leadership and Development Training. She is also co-owner and Chief Training Development Officer for Leaders in Transformational Education (LITE), an organization dedicated to serving youth in Chicago's local communities with life planning and career readiness. Sandra has a background in youth social services, community-based programming and drug and violence prevention. She is the proud mother of six children, and sixteen grandchildren. She and her devoted husband, Darryl Harrison Sr., have been married for over thirty years.

Dr. Tanya Sorrell

Tanya Sorrell, PhD, PMHNP-BC, is an Associate Professor at Rush University Medical Center. Dr. Sorrell has doctoral training in rural and urban underserved Mental Health and Substance use services research, and a minor in Complementary and Integrative Behavioral Health practices for Latino groups. She developed and taught a graduate nursing/medical course in Cultural Competence in Psychiatric assessment, diagnosis, and treatment, and provided course content/lectures to other students in mental health and cultural competency. This led to state and national accolades as she served on national SAMHSA committees for Cultural Competence in Nursing Care.

Na-Tae' Thompson

Na-Tae' Thompson is the co-founder of True Star Foundation, founded in 2004, which provides arts, culture, education training, employment and youth development services to Chicago youth. Students provide content for the digital platform truestar.life and learn skills in journalism, radio/podcast, digital marketing, graphic design, and marketing.

Sylvia Snowden

Sylvia Snowden is an award-winning broadcast journalist who has been with CAN TV for close to 14 years as the co-host of "Political Forum," editorial director for CAN TV Channel 42, membership recruiter, instructor, and non-profit services coordinator. Her freelance work has featured many outlets, including *The Huffington Post*, Ebony.com and *Jet Magazine*. She is the author of the blog, TrulySylvia.com.

Dena Chapman

Dena Chapman seeks to be a voice of strength and serenity in an otherwise noisy world. Dena is a freelance writer, editor, writing coach and a seasoned blogger. Currently, she is a contributing writer for *Bronzeville Life* (Chicago) and the Lead Editor for the Trinity United Church of Christ Devotion Writing Team. She co-authored, *How Do You Spell Win?* (2021) and to her credit has edited several books in an array of different genres. When Dena is not tinkering with words, she loves to get lost in the world of ballet and play with her Labrador-Retriever, Thor. Dena is the proud parent of two brilliant and beautiful young-adults, Joshua and Malachi.

Contact Dena @ precisionediting.org.

About The Author

Vee L. Harrison is an award-winning journalist from Chicago. Her work appears in publications across the city covering and highlighting Black culture and community news. Harrison is a Chicago change agent, setting the stage for new voices in Black media. During the course of her career as a journalist, Harrison has studied the city's racial segregation, politics, education and social structure through the lens of a Black woman raised in the city's largest, poorest community on the West Side during the 1990s.

Directly after receiving her B.A. from Columbia College, she served as a journalism instructor for inner-city youth in Chicago, promoting news literacy and Black-owned media. Harrison has spoken to over a dozen audiences across the nation.

Press coverage of her work as a Chicago media influencer can be found in the *Chicago Tribune*, WBEZ, WGN, iHeart Media, and from the city's mayor, Lori Lightfoot, where Harrison received recognition from the mayor during a televised press conference in May 2020. Harrison continues to cover community news in addition to Black fine arts and culture across the nation.

Harrison is the mother of five children and a Bichon Poodle.